Survey of
Credit Underwriting
Practices
2006

Office of the Comptroller of the Currency

October 2006

Contents

Introduction

The Office of the Comptroller of the Currency (OCC) conducted its twelfth annual survey of credit underwriting practices during the first quarter of 2006. The survey identified trends in lending standards and credit risk for the most common types of commercial and retail credit products offered by national banks.

The 2006 survey included results from the 73 largest national banks and covered the 12-month period ending March 31, 2006. Although mergers and acquisitions have altered the survey population, the survey has covered substantially the same group of banks for the past 10 years. All companies in the 2006 survey have assets of $2 billion or greater, and their aggregate loan portfolio was approximately $3 trillion as of year-end 2005, which represented over 90 percent of all outstanding loans in the national banking system.

The OCC examiners-in-charge of the surveyed banks were asked a series of questions concerning overall credit trends for 18 types of commercial and retail credit products. For purposes of this survey, the OCC groups commercial credit into 11 categories of loans: agricultural, asset-based, commercial construction, residential construction, other commercial real estate, commercial leasing, international, large corporate, leveraged, middle market, and small business. Retail credit consists of 7 categories of loans: affordable housing, credit card, indirect consumer paper (loans originated by others, such as car dealers), conventional home equity, high loan-to-value (HLTV) home equity, other direct consumer, and residential real estate mortgages.

The term "underwriting standards," as used in this report, refers to items such as collateral requirements, loan maturities, facility pricing, and covenants that banks establish when originating and structuring loans. Conclusions about "easing" or "tightening" of underwriting standards are drawn from the OCC examiners' judgment about observations since the 2005 survey. A conclusion that the underwriting standards for a particular loan category have eased or tightened does not indicate that all the standards for that particular category have been adjusted, or that all banks have eased standards. It indicates that the adjustments that did occur had the *net effect* of easing or tightening underwriting criteria.

Part I of this report summarizes the overall results of the survey. Part II depicts the survey results in graphs and tables.

Part I — Overall Results

Primary Findings

- *Competitive pressures have led to a third consecutive year of eased credit underwriting standards. Examiners report that national banks have eased underwriting standards for both commercial and retail credit products.*
- *Demand for bank loans from nonbank investors has influenced underwriting terms for leveraged loans and pushed credit spreads lower. The easing of standards for leveraged loans has extended more broadly to other types of commercial credit.*
- *While current loan performance and overall loan quality remain sound, credit risk is increasing due to the continued weakening of underwriting standards.*

Commentary on Credit Risk

The OCC's twelfth annual survey of credit underwriting practices indicates a third consecutive year of easing underwriting standards, as banks continue to stretch for volume and yield. While the current performance of commercial and retail portfolios remains sound, examiners note that credit risk has increased and is expected to continue to increase over the next 12 months.

While most of the easing has been noted in pricing concessions, there has also been easing in loan structure, such as tenor and guarantor requirements. Many OCC examiners commented on the liberalization of repayment terms and covenants. Of particular note is the increasing volume of term loans with nominal amortization required during the initial years of the exposure. The loosening of underwriting standards has been most dramatic in large corporate (syndicated credits) and leveraged loans, but spillover effects are also being seen in middle market lending as well. In commercial real estate, underwriting standards continue to loosen while concentrations continue to grow. Examiners noted that even when the applicable lending policy has not changed, the volume of exceptions to policy has increased.

Strong corporate earnings, a sustained economic expansion, abundant liquidity, and a global search for yield by institutional investors have led to significant investor appetite for bank-originated loans and lower credit spreads. A number of banks in the survey have increased their loan volumes through commercial syndications. Banks that purchase syndicated credits originated by other banks should recognize that the underwriting of these exposures often reflects the demand from nonbank institutional investors, many of whom have different investment horizons and greater risk tolerance than commercial banks. Such investors tend to prefer bond-like structures, with limited amortization requirements and fewer covenants. Originating banks may underwrite to these investor preferences and hold little of the originated exposure on their own balance sheet. The OCC reminds national banks of the need to follow the credit principles contained in Banking Circular 181 (REV), "Purchases of Loans in Whole or In Part — Participations," when purchasing loans. To make a prudent credit decision on a purchased loan, a national bank should conduct an independent credit analysis to satisfy itself that the credit exposure is one that it would assume directly. National banks that originate syndicated credits, on the other hand, should recognize that the quality of their originations may have reputation and liquidity risk implications.

Although asset quality performance of retail portfolios remains satisfactory, both delinquency levels and losses are beginning to show slight increases. Underwriting standards for retail credit continue to ease as banks aggressively seek market share. Reduced documentation requirements and more relaxed underwriting criteria are increasingly layered atop new products that can magnify risk levels, especially for unseasoned retail portfolios. Many borrowers have not yet been asked to perform under new, higher interest rates, or a principal-amortizing repayment structure.

A number of national bank chief credit officers have expressed concern to the OCC that competitive conditions, often from nonbank investors, have led to widespread weakening of underwriting standards and thin loan pricing. The OCC cautions national banks to evaluate and monitor the terms and conditions under which they extend credit. More specifically, the OCC encourages national banks to monitor and evaluate the volume of underwriting policy exceptions to determine the impact of loosening underwriting standards on credit quality. National banks should also ensure that weakening underwriting standards have not unduly compromised their tolerance for credit risk and that strong risk management systems exist to appropriately measure, monitor, and control the risks in their credit portfolios. National banks should review the risk management expectations set forth in the following OCC guidance:

- OCC Bulletin 2005-22, May 16, 2005, "Home Equity Lending — Credit Risk Management Guidance;"
- OCC Bulletin 2005-3, February 2, 2005, "Standards for National Banks' Residential Mortgage Lending Practices: OCC Guidelines;"
- OCC Bulletin 2003-1, January 8, 2003, "Credit Card Lending: Account Management and Loss Allowance Guidance;"
- OCC Bulletin 2001-18, April 9, 2001, "Leveraged Finance: Sound Risk Management Practice;" and
- Banking Circular 181 (REV), August 2, 1984, "Purchases of Loans in Whole or In Part — Participations."

Commercial Underwriting Standards

In 2006, the trend toward easing commercial credit standards continued, with significantly more banks easing than tightening standards. Examiners reported that 31 percent of banks eased overall commercial underwriting standards, compared to 34 percent in 2005. In 2006, only 6 percent tightened standards compared to 12 percent in 2005. The remaining 63 percent made no change to commercial underwriting standards. Notably, 43 percent of the banks eased standards in at least one of the past two years, with 18 percent of the banks easing standards in both years. The tightening of standards that prevailed during 1999–2003 began to turn in 2004 when examiners reported that 13 percent of banks eased and 12 percent tightened underwriting standards.

Underwriting trends at the product level confirm the broad easing trend in commercial loan products. Easing is most prevalent in large corporate/syndicated loans and leveraged lending. Sixty-two percent of the banks offering leveraged lending reported easing standards, nearly double the 2005 level. More than 30 percent of banks reported significant easing for commercial real estate and middle market loans. Since most banks offer these two products, the potential impact on credit quality and credit costs could be significant, supporting examiners' assessments of increasing credit risk. Examiners also noted that this is the third year of net easing for leveraged finance, asset-based lending, and middle market products.

Examiners again cited competition as the primary reason for easing commercial credit standards, and also pointed to significant liquidity in the marketplace, particularly from nonbank participants. As in prior years, the most common methods of easing standards were reduced pricing, increased advances, and lengthening tenors. For those banks that tightened standards, the primary reasons were a change in risk appetite and product performance. When tightening standards, banks relied on adjustments to covenants rather than collateral requirements as noted in last year's report.

Examiners reported that the level of credit risk in commercial portfolios has increased and is expected to continue increasing during the next 12 months. Examiners noted increased commercial credit risk in almost 30 percent of the sampled banks, with only 13 percent showing decreased risk. The greatest increase in risk was centered in commercial real estate products, leveraged lending, and large corporate loans.

Retail Underwriting Standards

For the second consecutive year, examiners noted easing of retail credit standards in more than a quarter of the banks surveyed. At the product level, easing was most notable in home equity lending and indirect consumer lending. Easing standards for home equity lending, both conventional and high loan-to-value, include longer interest-only periods, the offering of "piggy back" loans to avoid mortgage insurance requirements, lower scorecard cutoffs, and higher allowable debt-to-income and loan-to-value ratios.

Overall, "remaining competitive" is cited as the main reason for the easing of underwriting standards. The standards for home equity lending eased considerably further than indirect consumer lending, with the "easing" of indirect lending standards centered primarily in product changes, mainly longer terms. Examiners reported that 26 percent of the surveyed banks eased underwriting standards for residential mortgage lending, with an increased presence of nontraditional products such as interest-only loans and payment-option ARMs.

For the 7 percent of banks that tightened retail underwriting standards in 2006, a change in risk appetite was the primary rationale. Second was product performance, followed closely by regulatory guidance. The tightening was effected mainly through changes to scorecards, tighter debt service requirements, and more conservative minimum payment expectations. Credit card lending was cited most often as tightening standards (25 percent), attributed primarily to the implementation of higher minimum payments consistent with the account management guidance detailed in OCC Bulletin 2003-1, "Credit Card Lending: Account Management and Loss Allowance Guidance."

Examiners reported the level of retail credit risk increased in 25 percent of the banks since the prior survey, and they expect risk to increase in nearly a third of the banks over the next 12 months. Home equity lending led the retail products exhibiting higher risk levels. For conventional home equity products, examiners estimated increased risk in 31 percent of the reporting banks over the past year, and are forecasting increased risk in 49 percent of the banks over the next 12 months. For the 26 percent of surveyed banks reporting high loan-to-value home equity lending, examiners estimated increased risk in 37 percent of the banks over the past year, and are forecasting increased risk in 47 percent of the banks over the next 12 months. In general, examiners cite rising interest rates, concerns over a potential downturn in property values, and general portfolio seasoning for the increased risk levels. None of the banks exhibited decreasing risk for home equity products in the past year.

Part II — Graphs and Tables

Graphs

Commercial Product Tables

Retail Product Tables

Underwriting Trends for Commercial Credits

Percent of Banks

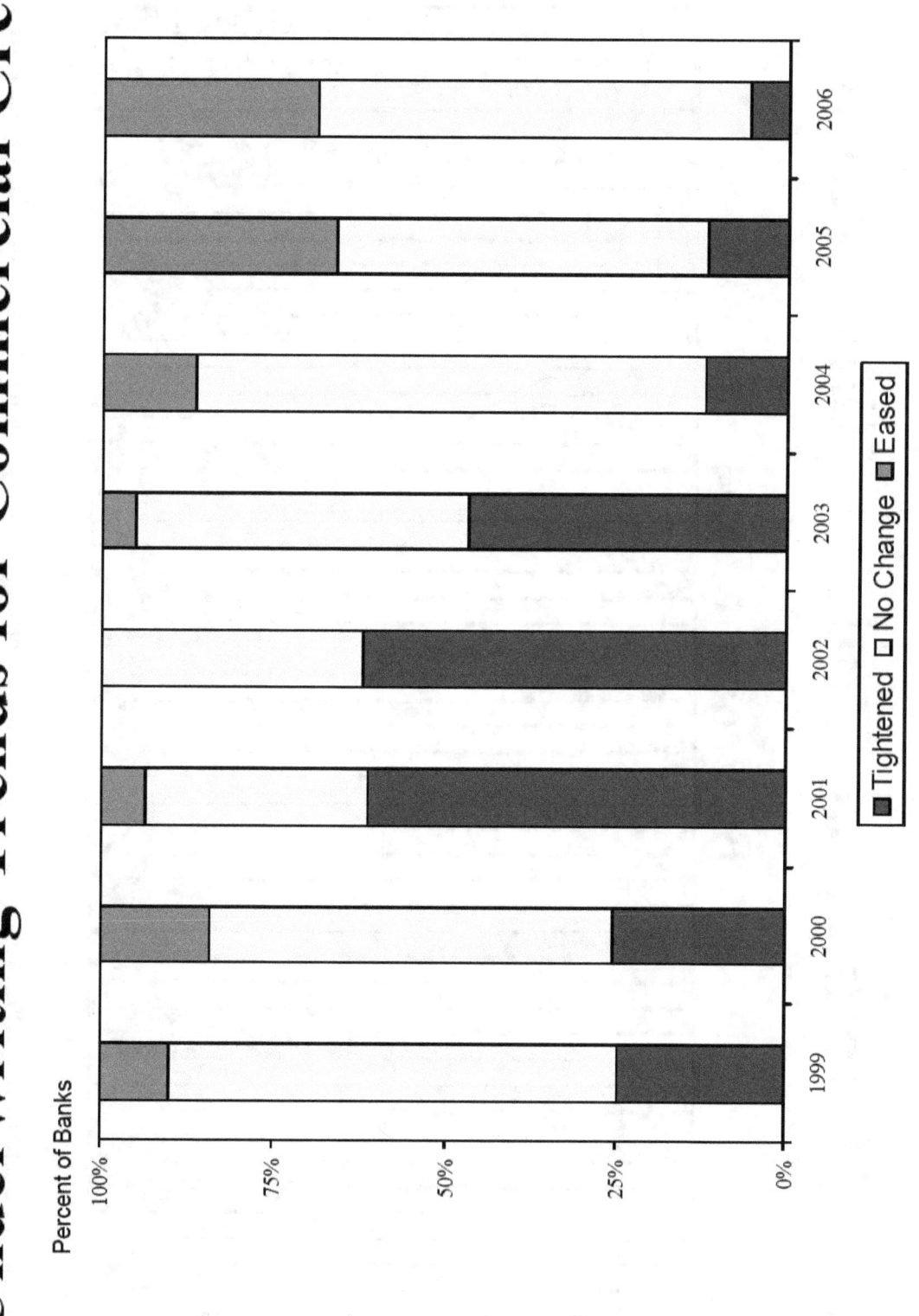

Legend: ■ Tightened □ No Change ■ Eased

Commercial Underwriting Trends

By Product Type

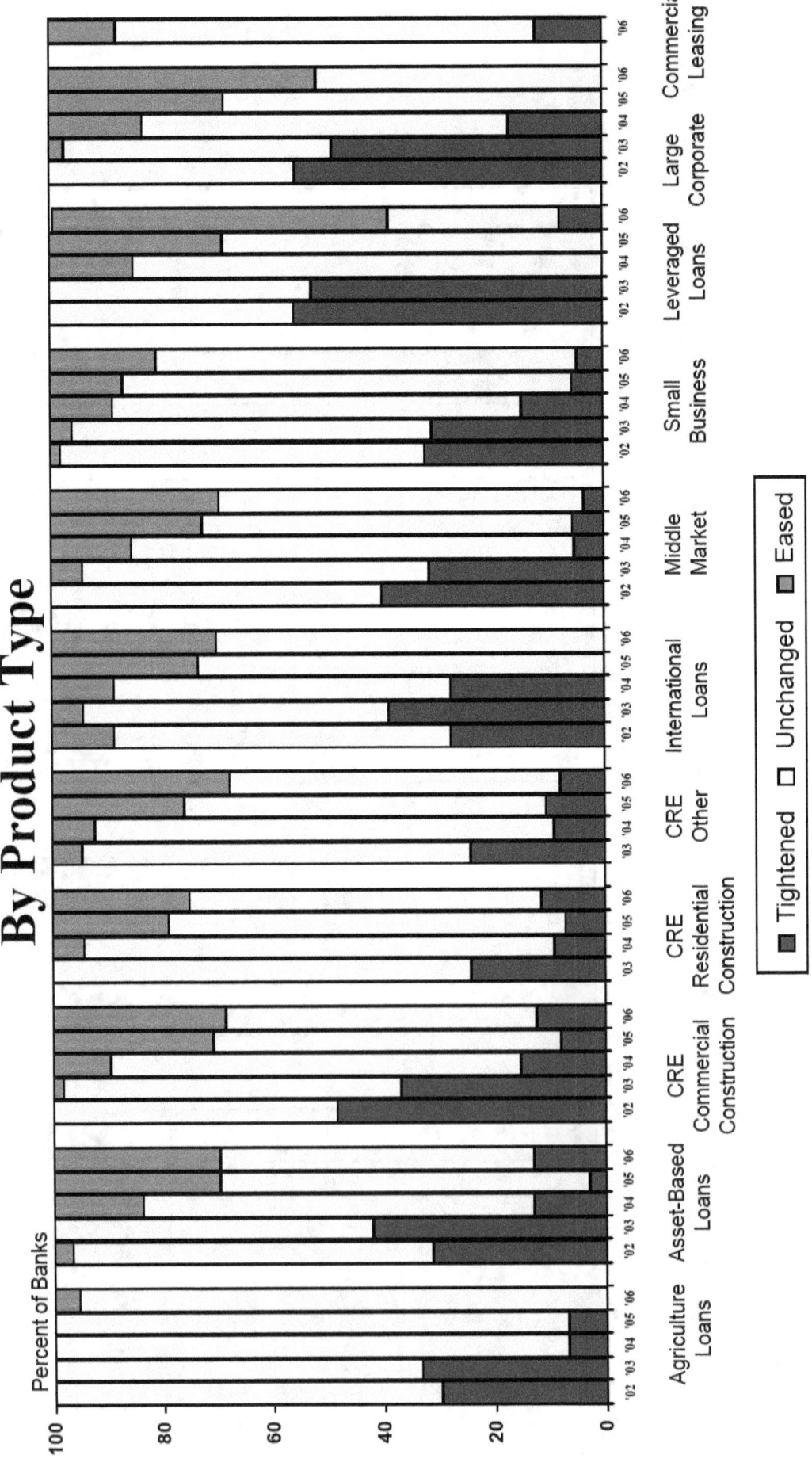

Reasons for Changing
Commercial Underwriting Standards

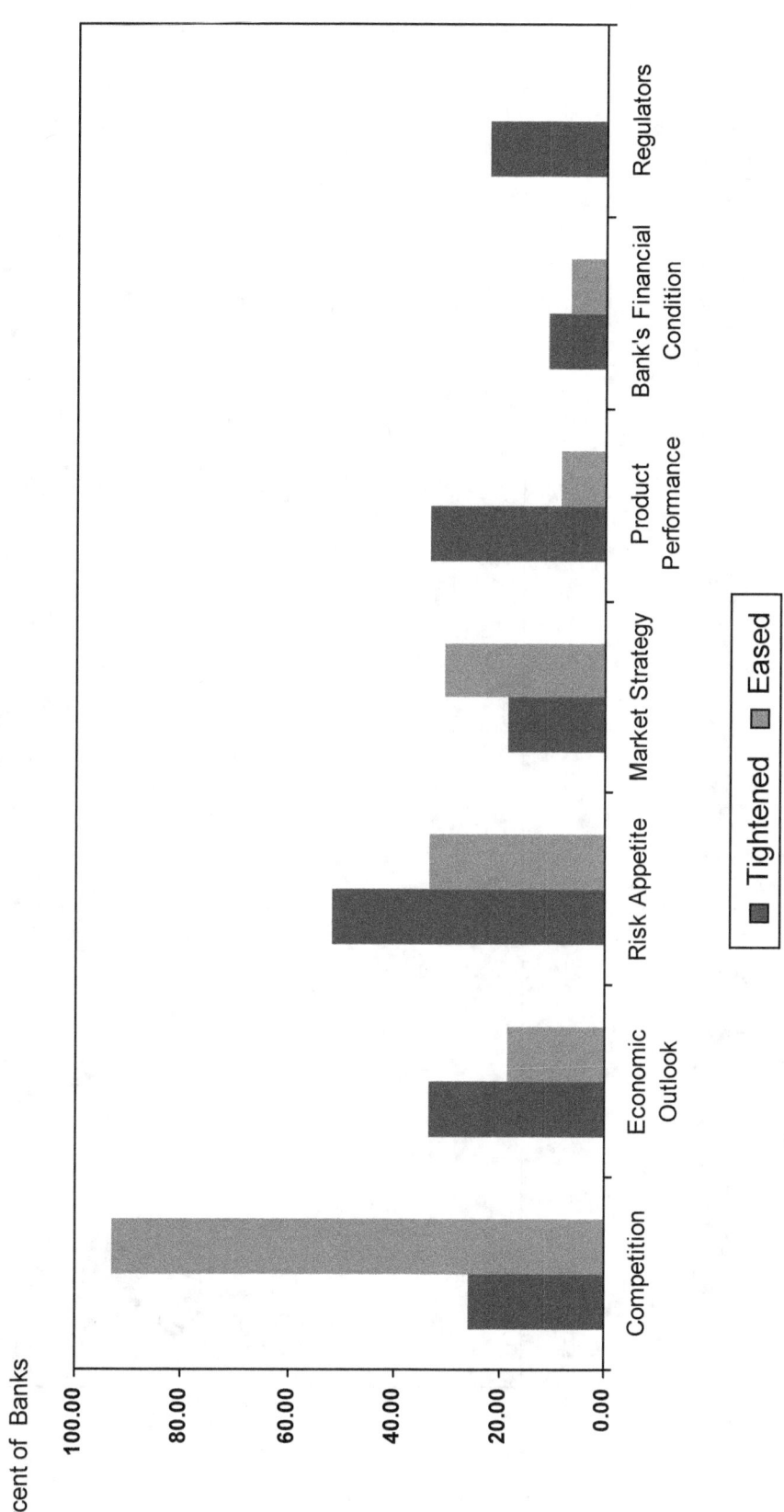

Percent of Banks

Methods Used to Change
Commercial Underwriting Standards

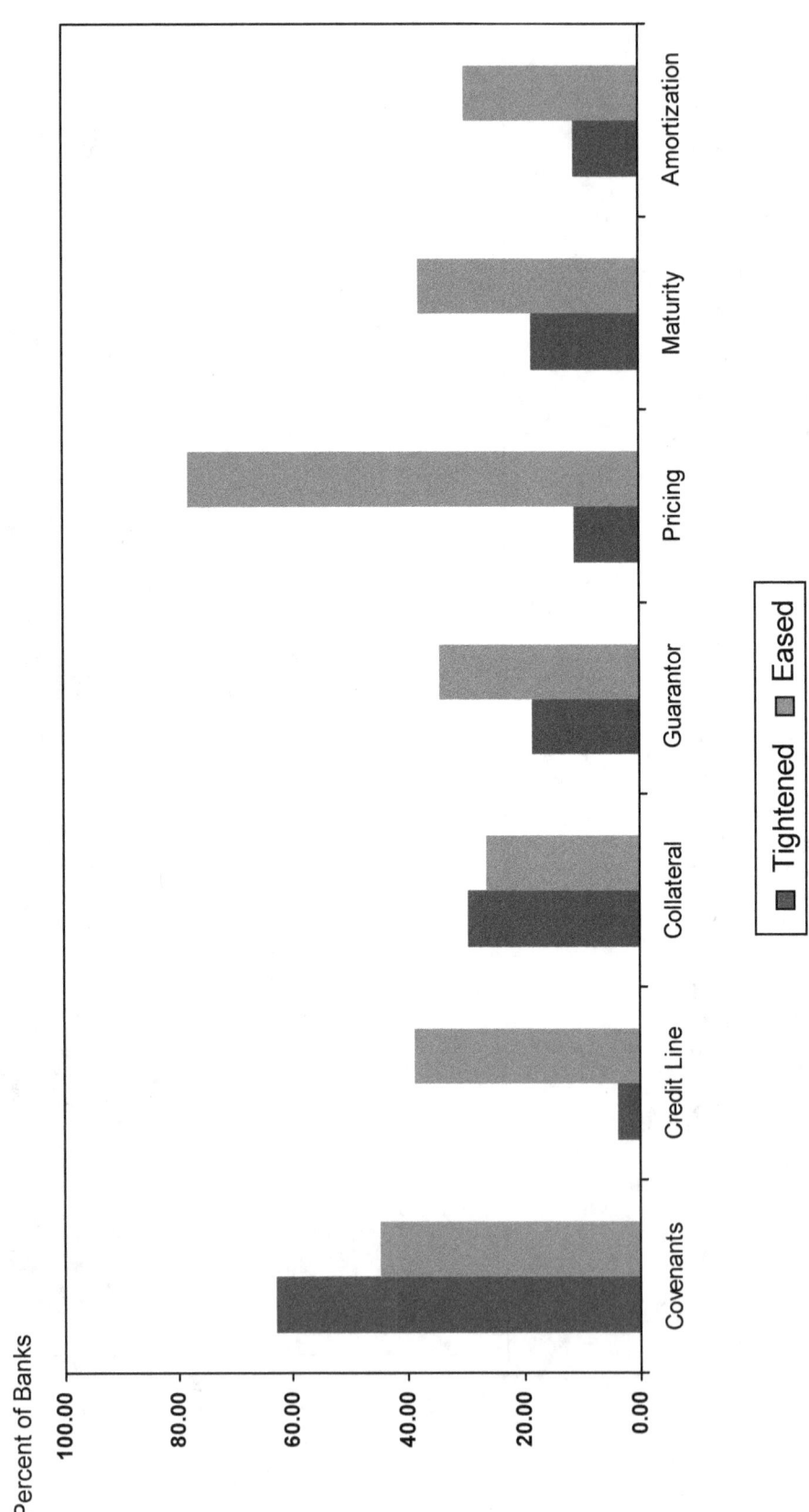

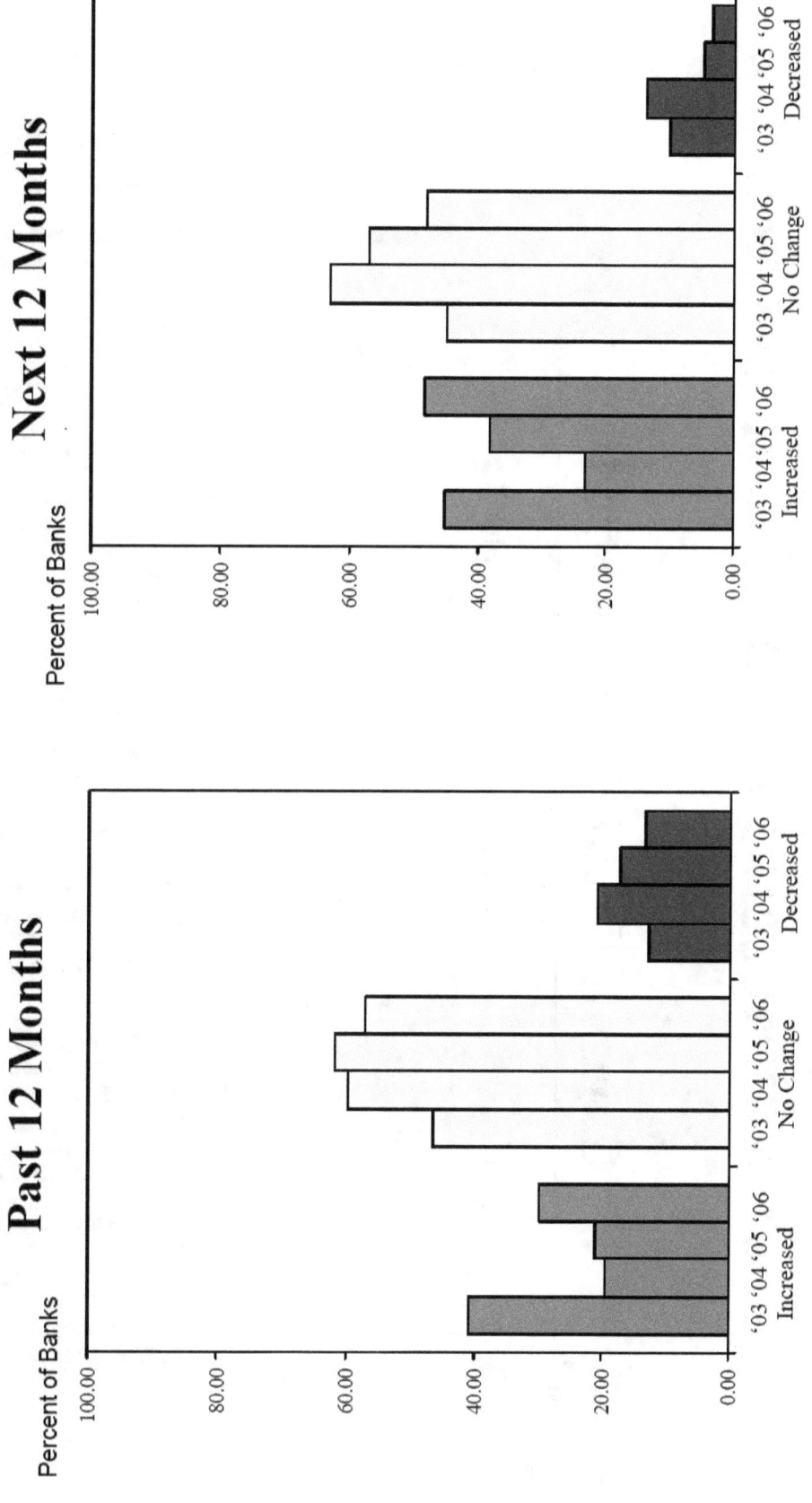

Commercial Credit Risk Trends

Current Credit Risk By Product Type

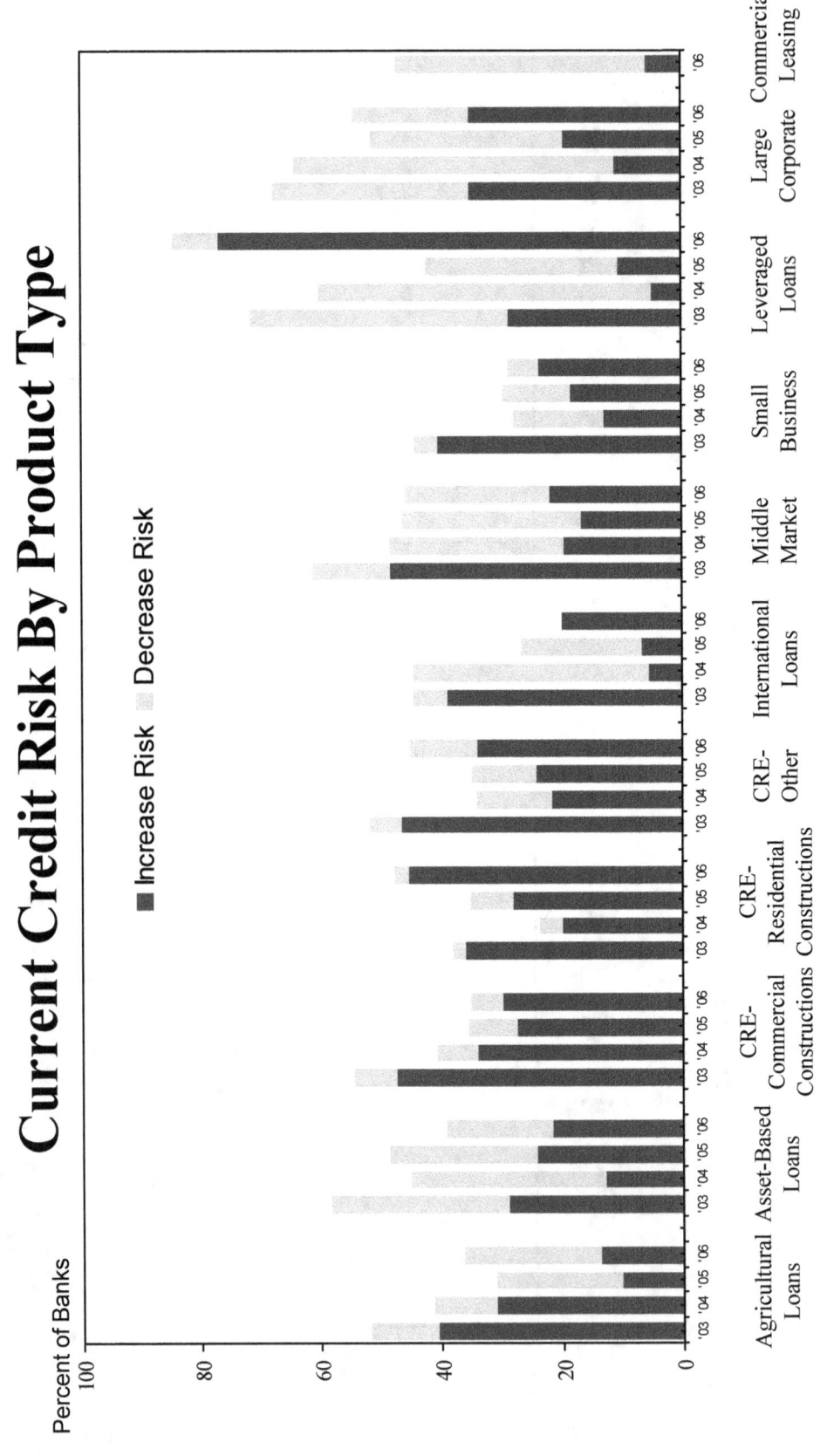

Underwriting Trends for Retail Credit

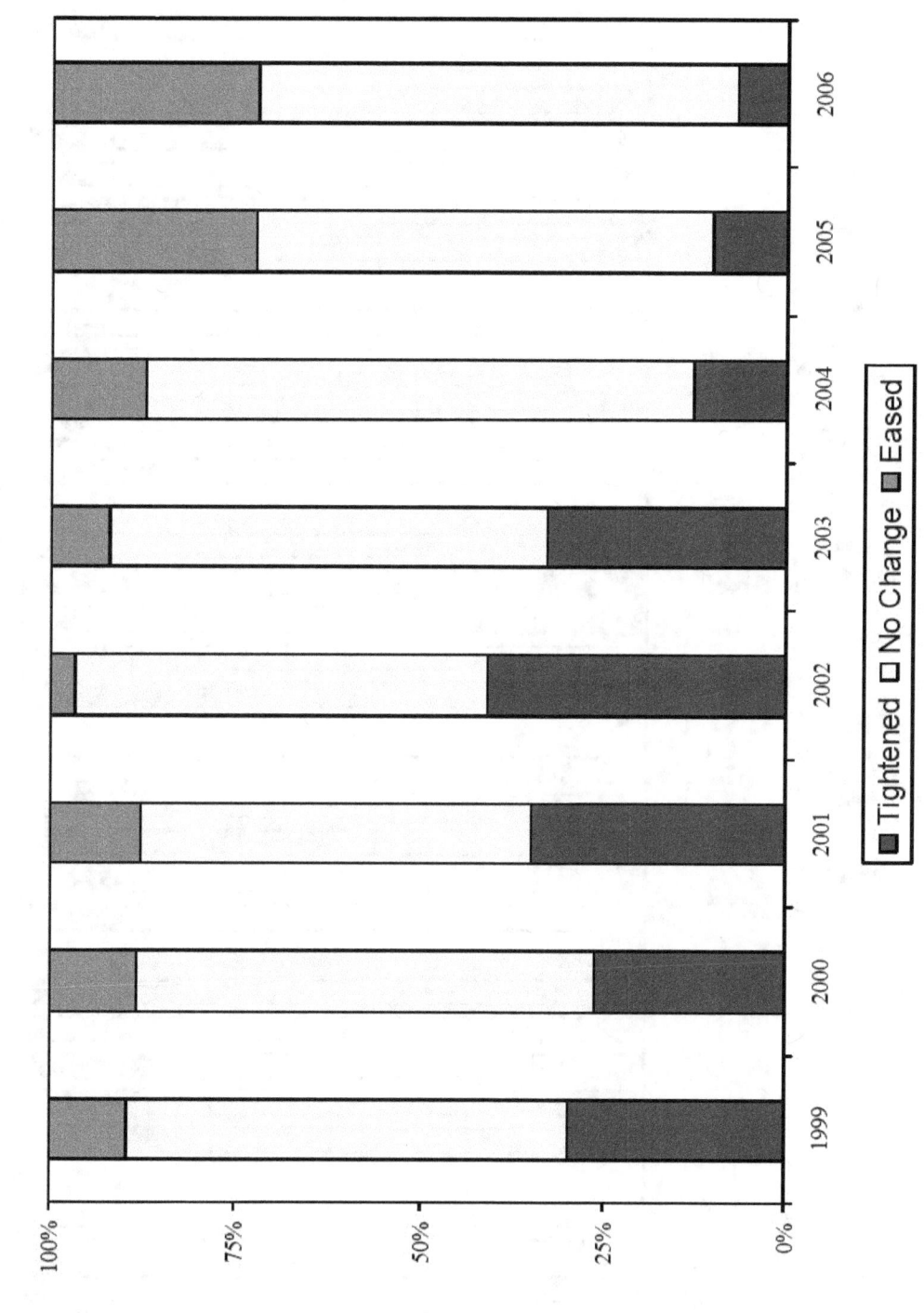

Retail Underwriting Trends

By Product Type

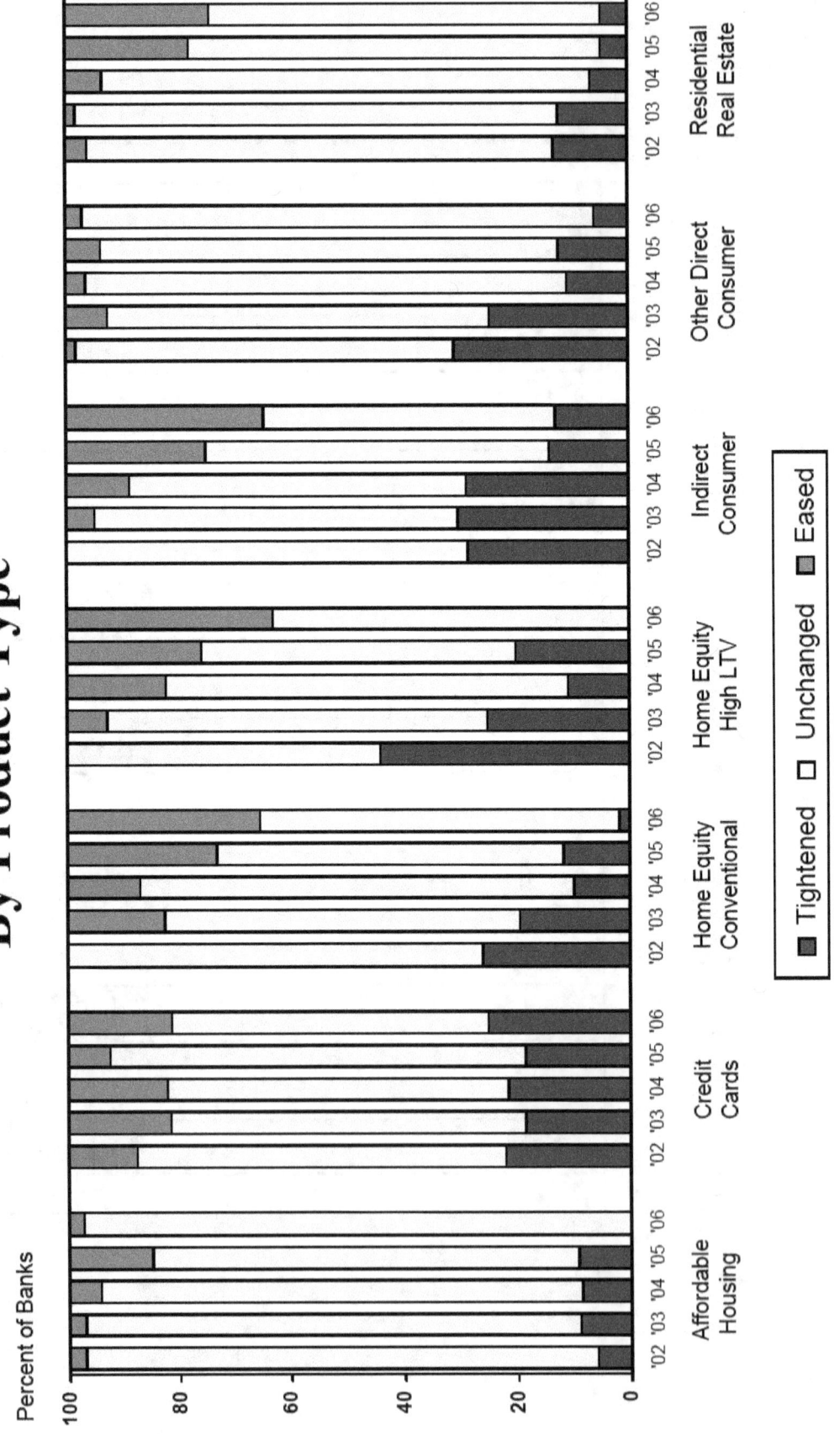

Percent of Banks

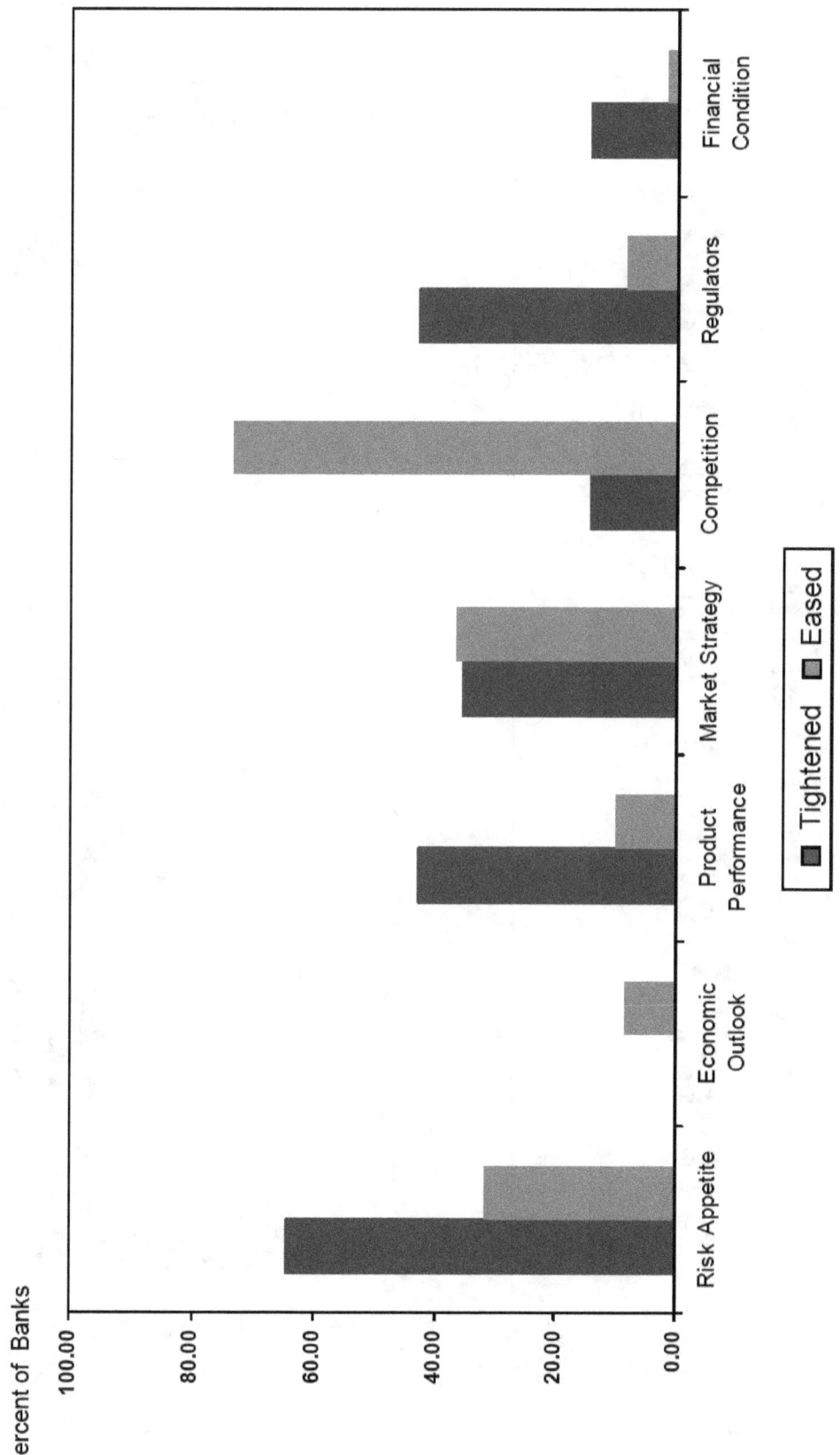

Reasons for Changing Retail Underwriting Standards

Methods Used to Change
Retail Underwriting Standards

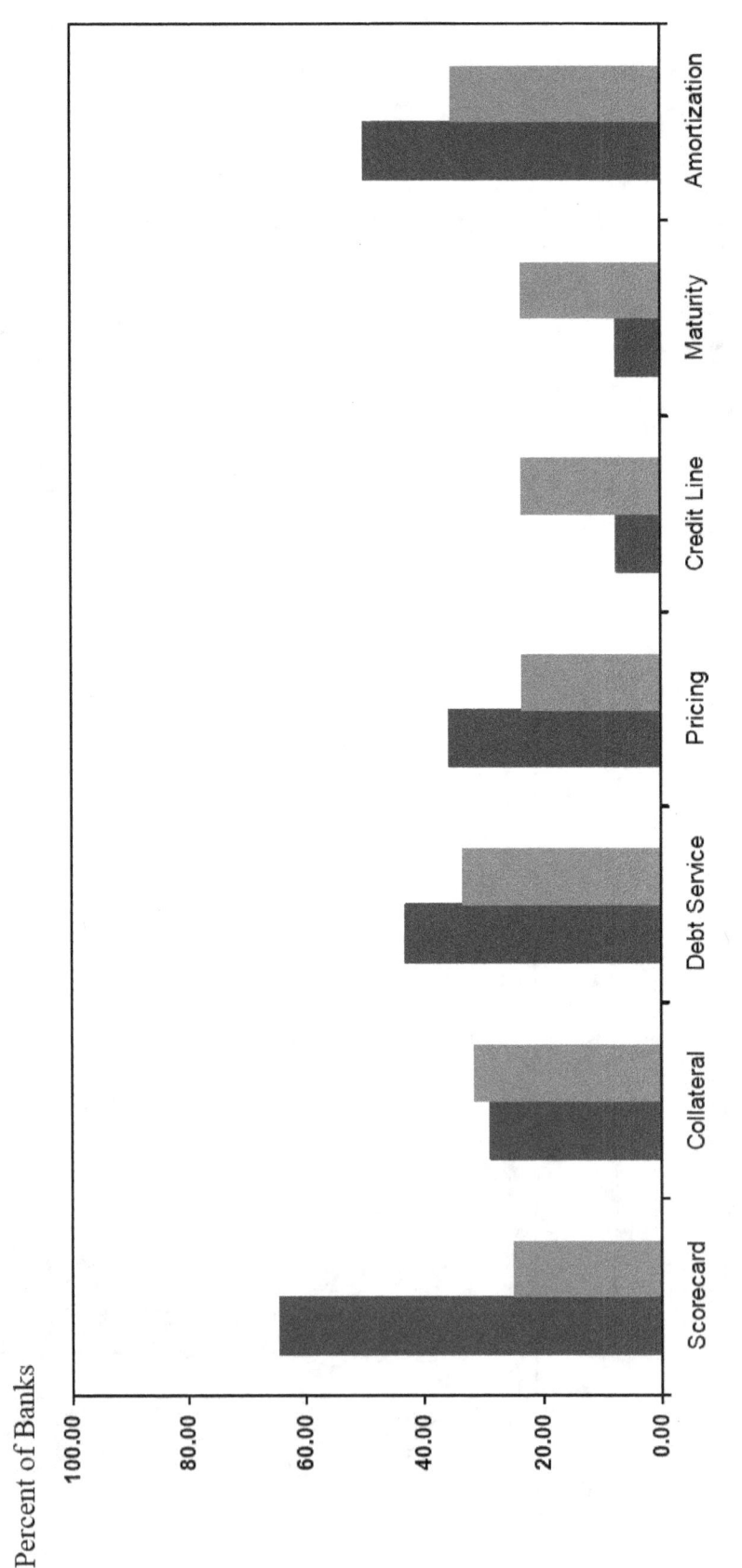

Percent of Banks

Retail Credit Risk Trends

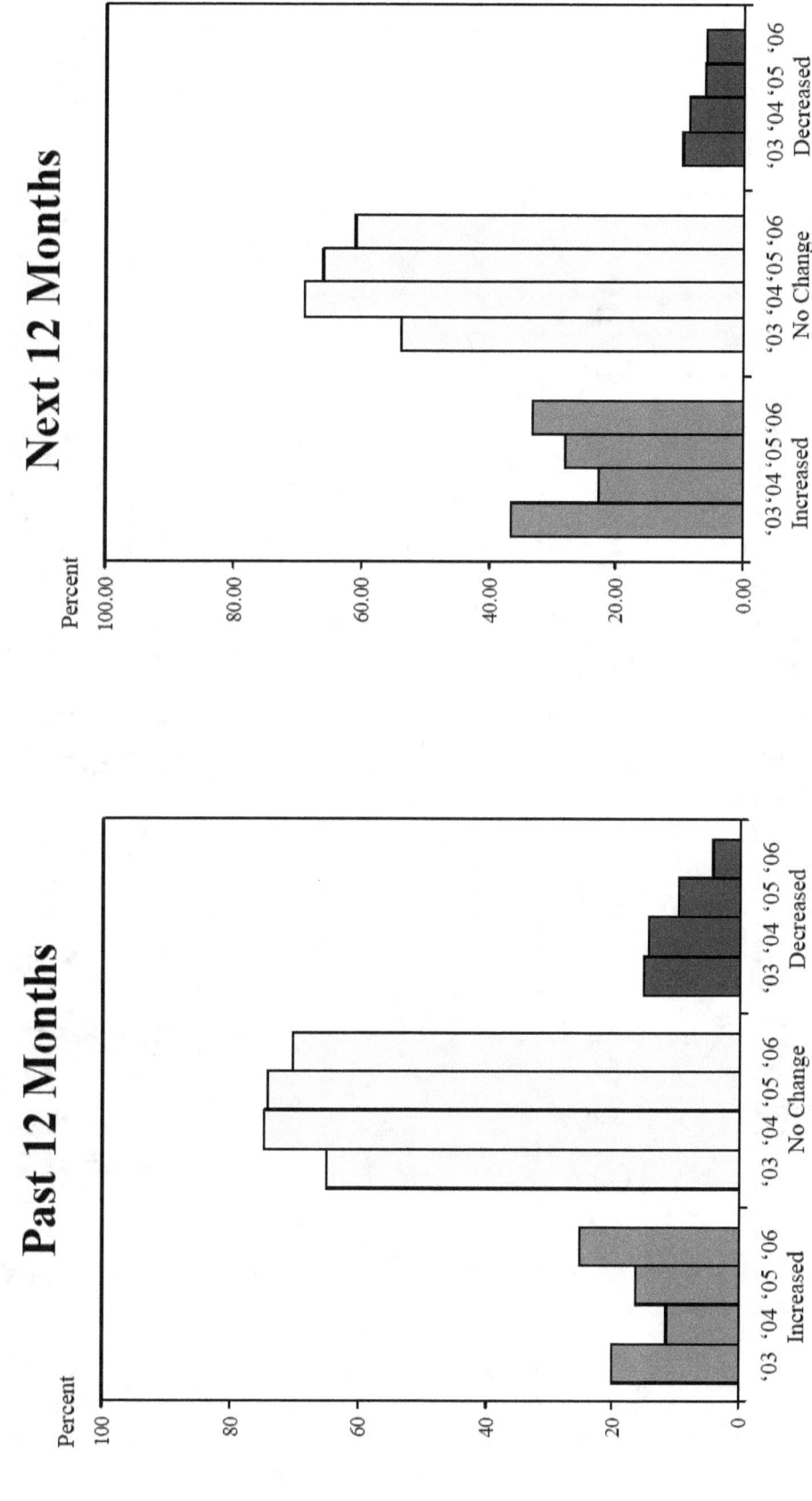

Retail Credit Risk Trends

Current Credit Risk By Product Type

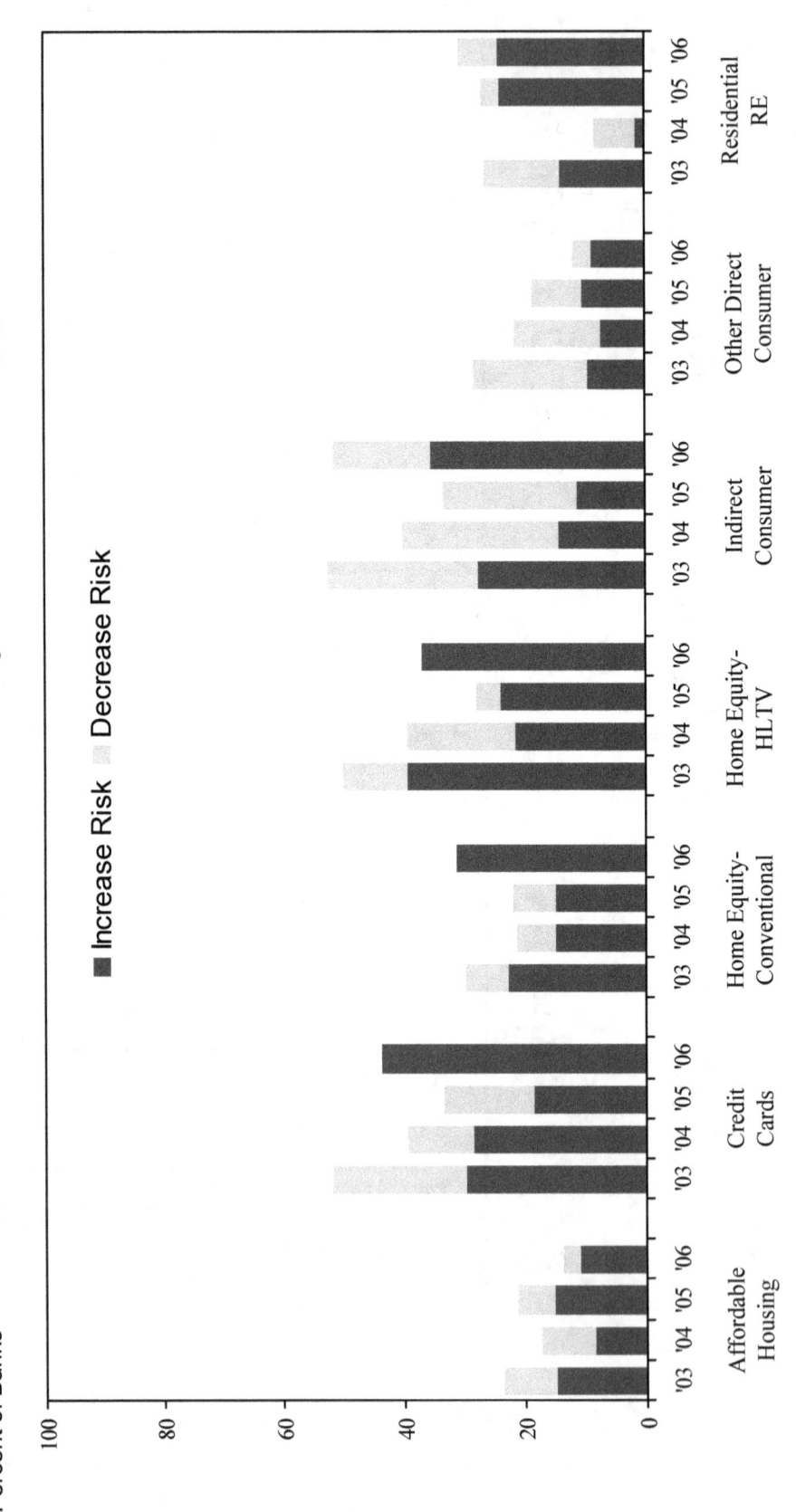

2006 Underwriting Survey

Tables

October 2006

Commercial Lending Portfolios

Agricultural Lending

Twenty-two of the 73 banks in the survey were engaged in some form of agricultural lending.

Changes in Underwriting Standards in Agricultural Loan Portfolios
(Percent of Banks)

	Eased	Unchanged	Tightened
1999	3	79	18
2000	3	71	26
2001	3	71	26
2002	0	70	30
2003	0	67	33
2004	0	93	7
2005	0	93	7
2006	5	95	0

Changes in the Level of Credit Risk in Agricultural Loan Portfolios
(Percent of Banks)

	Declined Significantly	Declined Somewhat	Unchanged	Increased Somewhat	Increased Significantly
1999	0	6	42	49	3
2000	0	15	41	44	0
2001	0	17	43	34	6
2002	0	7	63	30	0
2003	0	11	48	41	0
2004	0	10	59	31	0
2005	4	17	69	10	0
2006	0	23	63	14	0
Future 12 Months	0	9	59	32	0

Asset-Based Loans

Twenty-three of the 73 banks in the survey were engaged in asset-based lending.

Changes in Underwriting Standards in Asset-Based Loan Portfolios
(Percent of Banks)

	Eased	Unchanged	Tightened
1999	10	78	12
2000	11	67	22
2001	5	53	42
2002	3	66	31
2003	0	58	42
2004	16	71	13
2005	30	67	3
2006	30	57	13

Changes in the Level of Credit Risk in Asset-Based Loan Portfolios
(Percent of Banks)

	Declined Significantly	Declined Somewhat	Unchanged	Increased Somewhat	Increased Significantly
1999	0	10	66	24	0
2000	0	8	62	30	0
2001	5	8	42	45	0
2002	0	0	50	50	0
2003	3	26	42	29	0
2004	3	29	55	13	0
2005	0	24	52	24	0
2006	0	17	61	22	0
Future 12 Months	0	0	65	35	0

Commercial Leasing

Commercial leasing was offered by seventeen of the 73 banks in the survey.

Changes in Underwriting Standards in Commercial Leasing Portfolios
(Percent of Banks)

	Eased	Unchanged	Tightened
2006	12	76	12

Changes in the Level of Credit Risk in Commercial Leasing Portfolios
(Percent of Banks)

	Declined Significantly	Declined Somewhat	Unchanged	Increased Somewhat	Increased Significantly
2006	6	35	53	6	0
Future 12 Months	0	6	53	41	0

Commercial Real Estate Lending — Commercial Construction

Fifty-seven of the 73 banks in the survey were engaged in commercial construction lending.

Changes in Underwriting Standards in Commercial Construction Loan Portfolios
(Percent of Banks)

	Eased	Unchanged	Tightened
2003	2	61	37
2004	10	75	15
2005	29	63	8
2006	32	56	12

Changes in the Level of Credit Risk in Commercial Construction Loan Portfolios
(Percent of Banks)

	Declined Significantly	Declined Somewhat	Unchanged	Increased Somewhat	Increased Significantly
2003	0	7	46	42	5
2004	0	7	59	34	0
2005	2	5	65	28	0
2006	0	5	65	30	0
Future 12 Months	0	5	40	55	0

Commercial Real Estate Lending — Residential Construction

Forty-four of the 73 banks in the survey were engaged in residential construction lending.

Changes in Underwriting Standards in Residential Construction Loan Portfolios
(Percent of Banks)

	Eased	Unchanged	Tightened
2003	0	76	24
2004	5	86	9
2005	21	72	7
2006	25	64	11

Changes in the Level of Credit Risk in Residential Construction Loan Portfolios
(Percent of Banks)

	Declined Significantly	Declined Somewhat	Unchanged	Increased Somewhat	Increased Significantly
2003	0	2	62	34	2
2004	0	4	76	18	2
2005	2	6	65	27	0
2006	0	2	52	46	0
Future 12 Months	0	0	36	64	0

Commercial Real Estate Lending — Other

Sixty-two of the 73 banks in the survey were engaged in other commercial real estate lending.

Changes in Underwriting Standards in Other Commercial Real Estate Loan Portfolios
(Percent of Banks)

	Eased	Unchanged	Tightened
2003	5	71	24
2004	8	83	9
2005	24	65	11
2006	32	60	8

Changes in the Level of Credit Risk in Other Commercial Real Estate Loan Portfolios
(Percent of Banks)

	Declined Significantly	Declined Somewhat	Unchanged	Increased Somewhat	Increased Significantly
2003	0	5	48	43	4
2004	0	12	66	20	2
2005	2	9	65	24	0
2006	1	10	55	34	0
Future 12 Months	0	2	50	48	0

International Lending

Only ten of the 73 banks in the survey were active in international lending.

Changes in Underwriting Standards in International Loan Portfolios
(Percent of Banks)

	Eased	Unchanged	Tightened
1999	4	54	42
2000	14	72	14
2001	29	57	14
2002	11	61	28
2003	6	55	39
2004	11	61	28
2005	27	73	0
2006	30	70	0

Changes in the Level of Credit Risk in International Loan Portfolios
(Percent of Banks)

	Declined Significantly	Declined Somewhat	Unchanged	Increased Somewhat	Increased Significantly
1999	8	8	42	38	4
2000	0	33	53	14	0
2001	0	14	53	33	0
2002	0	22	39	28	11
2003	0	6	55	33	6
2004	6	33	55	6	0
2005	0	20	73	7	0
2006	0	0	80	20	0
Future 12 Months	0	0	70	30	0

Middle Market Lending

Fifty-nine of the 73 banks in the survey were engaged in middle market lending.

Changes in Underwriting Standards in Middle Market Loan Portfolios
(Percent of Banks)

	Eased	Unchanged	Tightened
1999	18	73	9
2000	18	66	16
2001	11	48	41
2002	0	60	40
2003	6	63	31
2004	14	81	5
2005	28	67	5
2006	31	66	3

Changes in the Level of Credit Risk in Middle Market Loan Portfolios
(Percent of Banks)

	Declined Significantly	Declined Somewhat	Unchanged	Increased Somewhat	Increased Significantly
1999	0	8	56	36	0
2000	0	2	50	46	2
2001	0	2	35	59	4
2002	2	8	22	66	2
2003	0	13	39	44	4
2004	0	28	52	18	2
2005	4	26	54	16	0
2006	0	24	54	20	2
Future 12 Months	0	5	51	42	2

Small Business Lending

Forty-two of the 73 banks in the survey are lending in the small business market.

Changes in Underwriting Standards in Small Business Loan Portfolios
(Percent of Banks)

	Eased	Unchanged	Tightened
1999	13	75	12
2000	8	73	19
2001	5	63	32
2002	2	66	32
2003	4	65	31
2004	11	74	15
2005	13	81	6
2006	19	76	5

Changes in the Level of Credit Risk in Small Business Loan Portfolios
(Percent of Banks)

	Declined Significantly	Declined Somewhat	Unchanged	Increased Somewhat	Increased Significantly
1999	0	8	67	23	2
2000	0	3	72	22	3
2001	0	3	60	37	0
2002	0	2	56	40	2
2003	0	4	56	38	2
2004	0	15	72	13	0
2005	0	11	70	19	0
2006	0	5	71	22	2
Future 12 Months	0	7	57	34	2

Leveraged Loans

Thirteen of the 73 banks in the survey provided leveraged loans.

Changes in Underwriting Standards in Leveraged Loan Portfolios
(Percent of Banks)

	Eased	Unchanged	Tightened
1999	24	44	32
2000	35	45	20
2001	0	4	96
2002	0	44	56
2003	0	48	52
2004	15	85	0
2005	32	68	0
2006	61	31	8

Changes in the Level of Credit Risk in Leveraged Loan Portfolios
(Percent of Banks)

	Declined Significantly	Declined Somewhat	Unchanged	Increased Somewhat	Increased Significantly
1999	0	4	36	56	4
2000	0	0	20	80	0
2001	0	4	8	46	42
2002	0	7	26	52	15
2003	10	33	28	29	0
2004	15	40	40	5	0
2005	5	27	58	5	5
2006	0	8	15	69	8
Future 12 Months	0	0	15	77	8

Large Corporate Loans

Thirty-seven of the 73 banks in the survey were active in large corporate loan market.

Changes in Underwriting Standards in Large Corporate Loan Portfolios
(Percent of Banks)

	Eased	Unchanged	Tightened
1999	18	50	32
2000	22	61	17
2001	0	34	66
2002	0	45	55
2003	3	49	48
2004	17	66	17
2005	32	68	0
2006	49	51	0

Changes in the Level of Credit Risk in Large Corporate Loan Portfolios
(Percent of Banks)

	Declined Significantly	Declined Somewhat	Unchanged	Increased Somewhat	Increased Significantly
1999	0	0	45	45	10
2000	0	0	36	61	3
2001	0	6	17	63	14
2002	0	8	29	53	10
2003	5	27	33	30	5
2004	17	36	36	11	0
2005	5	27	49	19	0
2006	0	19	46	32	3
Future 12 Months	0	0	43	57	0

Retail Lending Portfolios

Affordable Housing Lending

Affordable housing loans include all types of loans on affordable housing for low- and moderate-income individuals and families, including single- to four-family and multifamily dwellings. Thirty-seven of the 73 banks in the survey were reported to be making affordable housing loans.

Changes in Underwriting Standards in Affordable Housing Loan Portfolios
(Percent of Banks)

	Eased	Unchanged	Tightened
1999	16	70	14
2000	10	84	6
2001	6	88	6
2002	3	91	6
2003	3	88	9
2004	6	86	8
2005	15	76	9
2006	3	97	0

Changes in the Level of Credit Risk in Affordable Housing Loan Portfolios
(Percent of Banks)

	Declined Significantly	Declined Somewhat	Unchanged	Increased Somewhat	Increased Significantly
1999	2	2	78	18	0
2000	0	6	83	11	0
2001	2	2	88	8	0
2002	0	6	73	21	0
2003	0	9	76	15	0
2004	0	9	82	9	0
2005	0	6	79	15	0
2006	0	3	86	11	0
Future 12 Months	0	0	84	16	0

Credit Card Lending

Sixteen of the 73 banks in the survey banks were engaged in credit card lending.

Changes in Underwriting Standards in Credit Card Loan Portfolios
(Percent of Banks)

	Eased	Unchanged	Tightened
1999	8	66	26
2000	9	75	16
2001	16	60	24
2002	12	66	22
2003	19	62	19
2004	18	61	21
2005	7	74	19
2006	19	56	25

Changes in the Level of Credit Risk in Credit Card Loan Portfolios
(Percent of Banks)

	Declined Significantly	Declined Somewhat	Unchanged	Increased Somewhat	Increased Significantly
1999	0	13	47	36	4
2000	0	16	66	16	2
2001	8	5	57	27	3
2002	0	6	54	31	9
2003	0	22	48	30	0
2004	0	11	61	25	3
2005	0	15	67	18	0
2006	0	0	56	44	0
Future 12 Months	0	6	69	25	0

Direct Consumer Lending

Thirty-four of the 73 banks in the survey were engaged in direct consumer lending.

Changes in Underwriting Standards in Other Direct Consumer Loan Portfolios
(Percent of Banks)

	Eased	Unchanged	Tightened
1999	7	74	19
2000	10	78	12
2001	7	73	20
2002	2	67	31
2003	8	68	24
2004	3	86	11
2005	6	82	12
2006	3	91	6

Changes in the Level of Credit Risk in Other Direct Consumer Loan Portfolios
(Percent of Banks)

	Declined Significantly	Declined Somewhat	Unchanged	Increased Somewhat	Increased Significantly
1999	0	7	65	28	0
2000	0	9	74	15	2
2001	0	7	71	20	2
2002	2	6	67	25	0
2003	2	17	72	7	2
2004	2	13	78	7	0
2005	0	8	82	10	0
2006	0	3	88	9	0
Future 12 Months	0	6	82	12	0

Home Equity — Conventional Lending

Sixty-one of the 73 banks in the survey offered the conventional home equity lending product.

Changes in Underwriting Standards in Home Equity — Conventional Loan Portfolios
(Percent of Banks)

	Eased	Unchanged	Tightened
1999	23	67	10
2000	23	64	13
2001	7	70	23
2002	0	74	26
2003	18	63	19
2004	13	77	10
2005	27	62	11
2006	34	64	2

Changes in the Level of Credit Risk in Home Equity — Conventional Loan Portfolios
(Percent of Banks)

	Declined Significantly	Declined Somewhat	Unchanged	Increased Somewhat	Increased Significantly
1999	0	0	69	29	2
2000	0	5	73	20	2
2001	0	11	74	13	2
2002	0	7	71	22	0
2003	4	4	69	23	0
2004	0	6	79	13	2
2005	0	7	78	15	0
2006	0	0	69	29	2
Future 12 Months	0	2	49	49	0

Home Equity — High LTV Lending

Nineteen of the 73 banks in the survey offered the high LTV home equity lending product.

Changes in Underwriting Standards in Home Equity — High LTV Loan Portfolios
(Percent of Banks)

	Eased	Unchanged	Tightened
1999	20	61	19
2000	21	55	24
2001	11	54	35
2002	0	56	44
2003	7	68	25
2004	18	71	11
2005	24	56	20
2006	37	63	0

Changes in the Level of Credit Risk in Home Equity — High LTV Loan Portfolios
(Percent of Banks)

	Declined Significantly	Declined Somewhat	Unchanged	Increased Somewhat	Increased Significantly
1999	0	6	47	44	3
2000	0	13	58	24	5
2001	5	11	62	16	6
2002	0	12	40	44	4
2003	0	11	50	36	3
2004	0	18	61	18	3
2005	0	4	72	24	0
2006	0	0	63	37	0
Future 12 Months	0	0	53	47	0

Indirect Consumer Lending

Thirty-one of the 73 banks in the survey were engaged in indirect consumer lending.

Changes in Underwriting Standards in Indirect Consumer Loan Portfolios
(Percent of Banks)

	Eased	Unchanged	Tightened
1999	7	56	37
2000	7	60	33
2001	7	63	30
2002	0	72	28
2003	5	65	30
2004	11	60	29
2005	25	61	14
2006	35	52	13

Changes in the Level of Credit Risk in Indirect Consumer Loan Portfolios
(Percent of Banks)

	Declined Significantly	Declined Somewhat	Unchanged	Increased Somewhat	Increased Significantly
1999	2	23	42	33	0
2000	7	16	55	22	0
2001	2	21	39	33	5
2002	3	13	38	43	3
2003	5	20	47	28	0
2004	0	26	60	14	0
2005	3	19	67	8	3
2006	6	10	48	36	0
Future 12 Months	3	16	45	33	3

Residential Real Estate Lending

Sixty-two of the 73 banks in the survey were engaged in residential real estate lending.

Changes in Underwriting Standards in Residential Real Estate Loan Portfolios
(Percent of Banks)

	Eased	Unchanged	Tightened
1999	14	77	9
2000	7	85	8
2001	12	72	16
2002	4	83	13
2003	2	86	12
2004	7	86	7
2005	22	73	5
2006	26	69	5

Changes in the Level of Credit Risk in Residential Real Estate Loan Portfolios
(Percent of Banks)

	Declined Significantly	Declined Somewhat	Unchanged	Increased Somewhat	Increased Significantly
1999	3	5	71	21	0
2000	0	3	83	12	2
2001	0	9	76	15	0
2002	0	8	68	24	0
2003	0	12	74	12	2
2004	0	6	92	2	0
2005	0	3	73	24	0
2006	0	7	69	24	0
Future 12 Months	0	8	56	36	0